THE BROWNING VERSION

A Play in One Act

by

Terence Rattigan

SAMUEL  FRENCH

LONDON

NEW YORK TORONTO SYDNEY HOLLYWOOD

ISBN 0 573 02025 6

Please see page vi for further copyright information.

THE BROWNING VERSION

Produced at the Phœnix Theatre, London, on September 8th, 1948, with the following cast of characters:

(*in the order of their appearance*)

JOHN TAPLOW	*Peter Scott*
FRANK HUNTER	*Hector Ross*
MILLIE CROCKER-HARRIS	*Mary Ellis*
ANDREW CROCKER-HARRIS	*Eric Portman*
DR FROBISHER	*Campbell Cotts*
PETER GILBERT	*Anthony Oliver*
MRS GILBERT	*Henryetta Edwards*

The Play produced by Peter Glenville

THE SCENE

The action passes in the sitting-room of the Crocker-Harris's flat at a Public School in the South of England

Time: About 6.30 p.m. of a day in July

COPYRIGHT INFORMATION

(See also page iv)

THE BROWNING VERSION

SCENE.—*The sitting-room in the Crocker-Harris's flat in a public school in the south of England. About 6.30 p.m. of a day in July.*

The building in which the flat is situated is large and Victorian, and at some fairly recent time has been converted into flats of varying size for masters, married and unmarried. The Crocker-Harris have the ground floor and their sitting-room is probably the biggest—and gloomiest—room in the house. It boasts, however, access (through a stained glass door L.) *to a small garden, and is furnished with chintzy and genteel cheerfulness. Another door, up* R., *leads into the hall and a third, up* C., *to the rest of the flat. The hall door is partially concealed by a screen. There is a large bay-window in the* L. *wall below the garden door. Near the window is a flat-topped desk with a swivel chair behind it and an upright chair on the other side. The fireplace is down* R. *Below it is an easy chair and a small table with a telephone. A settee stands in front of the fireplace at* R.C. *There is an oval dining-table with two chairs up* C. R. *of the door up* C. *is a sideboard; and against the wall* L. *of the door up* R. *is a hall-stand, in which some walking-sticks are kept. A small cupboard stands against the wall down* R.

(See the Ground Plan of the scene.)

When the CURTAIN *rises the room is empty. There are copies of "The Times" and the "Tatler" on the settee. We hear the front door opening and closing and immediately after there is a timorous knock on the door up* R. *After a pause the knock is repeated. The door opens and* JOHN TAPLOW *makes his appearance. He is a plain moon-faced boy of about sixteen, with glasses. He carries a book and an exercise-book. He is dressed in grey flannels, a dark blue coat and white scarf. He stands in doubt at the door for a moment, then goes back into the hall.*

TAPLOW (*off; calling*). Sir! Sir!

(*After a pause he comes back into the room, crosses to the garden door up* L. *and opens it.*)

(*He calls.*) Sir!

(*There is no reply.* TAPLOW, *standing in the bright sunshine at the door, emits a plaintive sigh, then closes it firmly and comes down* R. *of the desk on which he places the book, the notebook and a pen. He sits in the chair* R. *of the desk. He looks round the room. On the table* C. *is a small box of chocolates, probably the Crocker-Harris's ration for the month.* TAPLOW *rises, moves above the table and opens the box. He counts the number inside, and removes two. One of these he eats and the other, after a second's struggle, either with his conscience or his judgment of what he might be able to get away with, virtuously replaces in the box. He puts back the box on the table, and moves up* R. *to the hall-stand. He selects a walking-stick with a crooked handle, comes down* C., *and makes a couple of golf-swings, with an air of great concentration.* FRANK HUNTER *enters up* R. *and appears from behind the screen covering the door. He is a rugged young man—not perhaps quite as rugged as his deliberately-cultivated manner of ruthless honesty makes him appear, but wrapped in all the self-confidence of the popular master. He watches* TAPLOW, *whose back is to the door, making his swing.*)

FRANK (*coming down behind* TAPLOW). Roll the wrists away from the ball. Don't break them like that.

(*He puts his large hands over the abashed* TAPLOW'S.)

Now swing.

(TAPLOW, *guided by* FRANK'S *evidently expert hands, succeeds in hitting the carpet with more effect than before.*)

(*He breaks away* R. *of Taplow.*) Too quick. Slow back and stiff left arm. It's no good just whacking the ball as if you were the headmaster and the ball was you. It'll never go more than fifty yards if you do.

Get a rhythm. A good golf swing is a matter of aesthetics, not of brute strength.

(TAPLOW, *only half listening, is gazing at the carpet.*)

FRANK. What's the matter?

TAPLOW. I think we've made a tear in the carpet, sir.

(FRANK *examines the spot perfunctorily.*)

FRANK (*taking the stick from* TAPLOW). Nonsense. That was there already. (*He crosses up* R. *and puts the stick in the hallstand.*) Do I know you? (*He comes down* L. *of the settee to* R. *of* TAPLOW.)

TAPLOW. No, sir.

FRANK. What's your name?

TAPLOW. Taplow.

FRANK. Taplow? No, I don't. You're not a scientist, I gather.

TAPLOW. No, sir. I'm still in the lower fifth. I can't specialize until next term—that's to say if I've got my remove all right.

FRANK. Don't you know yet if you've got your remove?

TAPLOW. No, sir. Mr Crocker-Harris doesn't tell us the results like the other masters.

FRANK. Why not?

TAPLOW. Well, you know what he's like, sir.

FRANK (*moving away to the fireplace*). I believe there *is* a rule that form results should only be announced by the headmaster on the last day of term.

TAPLOW. Yes; but who else pays any attention to it—except Mr Crocker-Harris?

FRANK. I don't, I admit—but that's no criterion. So you've got to wait until tomorrow to know your fate, have you?

TAPLOW. Yes, sir.

FRANK. Supposing the answer is favourable—what then?

TAPLOW. Oh—science sir, of course.

FRANK (*sadly*). Yes. We get all the slackers.

TAPLOW (*protestingly*). I'm extremely interested in science, sir.

FRANK. Are you? I'm not. Not at least in the science I have to teach.

TAPLOW (*moving above the desk*). Well, anyway, sir, it's a good deal more exciting than this muck. (*He indicates the book he put on the desk.*)

FRANK. What is this muck?

TAPLOW. Aeschylus, sir. *The Agamemnon.*

FRANK (*moving to the* L. *end of the couch*). And your considered view is that *The Agamemnon* of Aeschylus is muck, is it?

TAPLOW. Well, no, sir. I don't think the play is muck—exactly. I suppose, in a way, it's rather a good plot, really; a wife murdering her husband and having a lover and all that. I only meant the way it's taught to us—just a lot of Greek words strung together and fifty lines if you get them wrong.

FRANK. You sound a little bitter, Taplow.

TAPLOW. I am rather, sir.

FRANK. Kept in, eh?

TAPLOW. No, sir. Extra work.

FRANK. Extra work—on the last day of school?

TAPLOW. Yes, sir—and I might be playing golf. (*He moves into the window, upstage end.*) You'd think *he'd* have enough to do anyway himself, considering he's leaving tomorrow for good—but oh no. I missed a day last week when I had 'flu—so here I am—and look at the weather, sir.

FRANK. Bad luck. Still there's one consolation. You're pretty well bound to get your remove tomorrow for being a good boy in taking extra work.

TAPLOW (*crossing to* C.). Well, I'm not so sure, sir. That would be true of the ordinary masters all right. They just wouldn't dare not give a chap a remove after his taking extra work—it would be such a bad advertisement for them. But those sort of rules don't apply to the Crock—Mr Crocker-Harris. I asked him yesterday outright if he'd given me a remove and do you know what he said, sir?

FRANK. No. What?

TAPLOW (*mimicking a very gentle, rather throaty voice*). " My dear Taplow, I have given you exactly what you deserve. No less ; and certainly no more." Do you know, sir, I think he may have marked me down, rather than up, for taking extra work. I mean, the man's barely human. (*He breaks off quickly.*) Sorry, sir. Have I gone too far?

FRANK (*sitting on the settee,* L. *end, and picking up " The Times "*). Yes. Much too far.

TAPLOW. Sorry, sir. I got sort of carried away.

FRANK. Evidently. (*He opens " The Times " and reads.*)

(TAPLOW *moves to the chair* R. *of the desk and sits.*)

Er—Taplow.

TAPLOW. Yes, sir?

FRANK. What was that Mr Crocker-Harris said to you? Just—er—repeat it, would you?

TAPLOW (*mimicking*). " My dear Taplow, I have given you exactly what you deserve. No less ; and certainly no more."

(FRANK *snorts, then looks stern.*)

FRANK. Not in the least like him. Read your nice Aeschylus and be quiet.

TAPLOW (*with weary disgust*). Aeschylus.

FRANK. Look, what time did Mr Crocker-Harris tell you to be here?

TAPLOW. Six-thirty, sir.

FRANK. Well, he's ten minutes late. Why don't you cut? You could still get nine holes in before lock-up.

TAPLOW (*genuinely shocked*). Oh, no, I couldn't cut. Cut the Crock—Mr Crocker-Harris? I shouldn't think it's ever been done in the whole time he's been here. God knows what would happen if I did. He'd probably follow me home, or something.

FRANK. I must admit I envy him the effect he seems to have on you boys in his form. You all seem scared to death of him. What does he do—beat you all, or something?

TAPLOW (*rising and moving to the* L. *end of the settee*). Good Lord, no. He's not a sadist, like one or two of the others.

FRANK. I beg your pardon?

TAPLOW. A sadist, sir, is someone who gets pleasure out of giving pain.

FRANK. Indeed? But I think you went on to say that some other masters . . .

TAPLOW. Well, of course they are, sir. I won't mention names, but you know them as well as I do. Of course I know most masters think we boys don't understand a thing—but dash it, sir, you're different. You're young—well comparatively anyway—and you're science and you canvassed for Labour in the last election. You must know what sadism is.

(FRANK *stares for a moment at* TAPLOW, *then turns away.*)

FRANK. Good Lord! What are public schools coming to?

TAPLOW (*crossing to* R. *of the desk, below the chair, and leaning against it*). Anyway, the Crock isn't a sadist. That's what I'm saying. He wouldn't be so frightening if he were—because at least it would show he had some feelings. But he hasn't. He's all shrivelled up inside like a nut and he seems to hate people to like him. It's funny, that. I don't know any other master who doesn't like being liked.

FRANK. And I don't know any boy who doesn't trade on that very foible.

TAPLOW. Well, it's natural, sir. But not with the Crock.

FRANK (*making a feeble attempt at re-establishing the correct relationship*). Mr Crocker-Harris.

TAPLOW. Mr Crocker-Harris. The funny thing is that in spite of everything, I do rather like him. I can't help it. And sometimes I think he sees it and that seems to shrivel him up even more.

FRANK. I'm sure you're exaggerating.

TAPLOW. No, sir. I'm not. In form the other day he made one of his little classical jokes. Of course nobody laughed because nobody understood it, myself included. Still, I knew he'd meant it as funny, so I laughed. Not out of sucking-up, sir, I swear, but ordinary common politeness, and feeling a bit sorry for him having made a dud joke. (*He moves round below the desk to* L. *of it.*) Now I can't remember what the joke was—but let's say it was—(*mimicking*) Benedictus, benedicatur, benedictine... Now, you laugh, sir.

(FRANK *laughs formally.* TAPLOW *looks at him over an imaginary pair of spectacles, and then, very gently crooks his fore-finger to him in indication to approach the table.* FRANK *rises. He is genuinely interested in the incident.*)

(*In a gentle, throaty voice.*) Taplow—you laughed at my little pun, I noticed. I must confess I am flattered at the evident advance your Latinity has made that you should so readily have understood what the rest of the form did not. Perhaps, now, you would be good enough to explain it to them, so that they too can share your pleasure.

(*The door up* R. *is pushed open and* MILLIE CROCKER-HARRIS *enters. She is a thin woman in the late thirties, rather more smartly dressed than the general run of schoolmasters' wives. She is wearing a cape and carries a shopping basket. She closes the door and then stands by the screen watching* TAPLOW *and* FRANK. *It is a few seconds before they notice her.*)

Come along, Taplow.

(FRANK *moves slowly above the desk.*)

Do not be so selfish as to keep a good joke to yourself. Tell the others . . . (*He breaks off suddenly, noticing* MILLIE.) Oh Lord !

(FRANK *turns quickly, and seems infinitely relieved at seeing* MILLIE.)

FRANK. Oh, hullo.

MILLIE (*without expression*). Hullo. (*She comes down to the sideboard and puts her basket on it.*)

TAPLOW (*moving up to* L. *of* FRANK; *whispering frantically*). Do you think she heard?

(FRANK *shakes his head comfortingly.* MILLIE *takes off her cape and hangs it on the hall-stand.*)

I think she did. She was standing there quite a time. If she did and she tells him, there goes my remove.

FRANK. Nonsense. (*He crosses to the fireplace.*)

(MILLIE *takes the basket from the sideboard, moves above the table* C. *and puts the basket on it.*)

MILLIE (*to* TAPLOW). Waiting for my husband?

TAPLOW (*moving down* L. *of the table* C.). Er—yes.

MILLIE. He's at the Bursar's and might be there quite a time. If I were you I'd go.

TAPLOW (*doubtfully*). He said most particularly I was to come.

MILLIE. Well, why don't you run away for a quarter of an hour and come back? (*She unpacks some things from the basket.*)

TAPLOW. Supposing he gets here before me?

MILLIE (*smiling*). I'll take the blame. (*She takes a prescription out of the basket.*) I tell you what—you can do a job for him. Take this prescription to the chemist and get it made up.

TAPLOW. All right, Mrs Crocker-Harris. (*He crosses towards the door up* R.)

MILLIE. And while you're there you might as well slip into Stewart's and have an ice. Here. Catch. (*She takes a shilling from her bag and throws it to him.*)

TAPLOW (*turning and catching it*). Thanks awfully. (*He signals to* FRANK *not to tell, and moves to the door up* R.)

MILLIE. Oh, Taplow. (*She crosses to him.*)

TAPLOW (*turning on the step*). Yes, Mrs Crocker-Harris.

MILLIE. I had a letter from my father today in

which he says he once had the pleasure of meeting your mother.

TAPLOW (*uninterested but polite*). Oh, really?

MILLIE. Yes. It was at some fête or other in Bradford. My uncle—that's Sir William Bartop, you know—made a speech and so did your mother. My father met her afterwards at tea.

TAPLOW. Oh really?

MILLIE. He said he found her quite charming.

TAPLOW. Yes, she's jolly good at those sort of functions. (*Becoming aware of his lack of tact.*) I mean—I'm sure she found him charming, too. So long.

(*He goes out up* R.)

MILLIE (*coming down to the* L. *end of the settee*). Thank you for coming round.

FRANK. That's all right.

MILLIE. You're staying for dinner?

FRANK. If I may.

MILLIE. If you may! (*She crosses below the settee to him.*) Give me a cigarette.

(FRANK *takes out his case and extends it to her.* MILLIE *takes a cigarette.*)

(*Indicating the case.*) You haven't given it away yet, I see.

FRANK. Do you think I would?

MILLIE. Frankly, yes. Luckily it's a man's case. I don't suppose any of your girl friends would want it.

FRANK. Don't be silly.

MILLIE. Where have you been all this week?

FRANK (*sitting in the easy chair*). Correcting exam papers—making reports. You know what end of term is like.

MILLIE (*crossing below the settee and moving above the table* C.). I do know what end of term is like. But even Andrew has managed this last week to take a few hours off to say good-bye to people. (*She takes some packages out of the shopping basket.*)

FRANK. I really have been appallingly busy. Besides, I'm coming to stay with you in Bradford.

MILLIE. Not for over a month. Andrew doesn't start his new job until September first. That's one of the things I had to tell you.

FRANK. Oh. I had meant to be in Devonshire in September.

MILLIE (*quickly*). Who with?

FRANK. My family.

MILLIE. Surely you can go earlier, can't you? Go in August.

FRANK. It'll be difficult.

MILLIE. Then you'd better come to me in August.

FRANK. But Andrew will still be there.

(*There is a pause.* MILLIE *crosses to* L. *of the desk, opens a drawer and takes out some scissors.*)

FRANK. I think I can manage September.

MILLIE (*shutting the drawer*). That'd be better—from every point of view. (*She moves below the table* C. *and puts down the scissors.*) Except that it means I shan't see you for six weeks.

FRANK (*lightly*). You'll survive that, all right.

MILLIE. Yes, I'll survive it—(*she moves to the* L. *end of the settee*) but not as easily as you will.

(FRANK *says nothing.*)

I haven't much pride, have I? (*She crosses to* FRANK *and stands above the easy chair.*) Frank, darling—(*she sits on the arm of the chair and kisses him*) I love you so much.

(FRANK *kisses her on the mouth, but a trifle perfunctorily, and then rises and breaks quickly away, as if afraid someone had come into the room. He moves below the settee.*)

(*She laughs.*) You're very nervous.

FRANK. I'm afraid of that screen arrangement. You can't see people coming in.

MILLIE. Oh yes. (*She rises and stands by the fire-

place.) That reminds me. What were you and Taplow up to when I came in just now? Making fun of my husband?

FRANK. Afraid so. Yes.

MILLIE. It sounded rather a good imitation. I must get him to do it for me sometime. It was very naughty of you to encourage him.

FRANK. I know. It was.

MILLIE (*ironically*). Bad for discipline.

FRANK (*sitting on the settee*). Exactly. Currying favour with the boys, too. My God, how easy it is to be popular. I've only been a master three years, but I've already slipped into an act and a vernacular that I just can't get out of. Why can't anyone ever be natural with the little blighters?

MILLIE. They probably wouldn't like it if you were. (*She crosses below the settee and moves above the table* C. *She picks up the scissors and a packet of luggage labels and cuts the latter one by one from the packet.*)

FRANK. I don't see why not. No one seems to have tried it yet, anyway. I suppose the trouble is— we're all too scared of them. Either one gets forced into an attitude of false and hearty and jocular bonhomie like myself, or into the sort of petty, soulless tyranny which your husband uses to protect himself against the lower fifth.

MILLIE (*rather bored with this*). He'd never be popular—whatever he did.

FRANK. Possibly not. He ought never to have become a schoolmaster really. Why did he?

MILLIE. It was his vocation, he said. He was sure he'd make a big success of it, especially when he got his job here first go off. (*Bitterly.*) Fine success he's made, hasn't he?

FRANK. You should have stopped him.

MILLIE. How was I to know? He talked about getting a house, then a headmastership.

FRANK (*rising*). The Crock a headmaster! That's a pretty thought.

MILLIE. Yes, it's funny to think of now, all right.

Still, he wasn't always the Crock, you know. He had a bit more gumption once. At least I thought he had. Don't let's talk any more about him—(*she comes* R. *round the table to* C.) it's too depressing. (*She starts to move* L.)

FRANK. I'm sorry for him.

MILLIE (*stopping and turning ; indifferently*). He's not sorry for himself, so why should you be ? It's me you should be sorry for.

FRANK. I am.

MILLIE (*moving in a few steps towards* FRANK ; *smiling*). Then show me. (*She stretches out her arms to him.*)

(FRANK *moves to her and kisses her again quickly and lightly. She holds him hungrily. He has to free himself almost roughly.*)

FRANK (*crossing to the fireplace*). What have you been doing all day ?

MILLIE. Calling on the other masters' wives—saying fond farewells. I've worked off twelve. I've another seven to do tomorrow.

FRANK. You poor thing ! I don't envy you.

MILLIE (*moving above the desk to* L. *of it with some labels*). It's the housemasters' wives that are the worst. (*She picks up a pen and writes on the labels.*) They're all so damn patronizing. You should have heard Betty Carstairs. " My dear—it's such terrible bad luck on you both—that your husband should get this heart trouble just when, if only he'd stayed on, he'd have been bound to get a house. I mean, he's considerably senior to my Arthur as it is, and they simply couldn't have gone on passing him over, could they ? "

FRANK. There's a word for Betty Carstairs, my dear, that I would hesitate to employ before a lady.

MILLIE. She's got her eye on you, anyway.

FRANK. Betty Carstairs ? What utter rot !

MILLIE. Oh yes, she has. I saw you at that concert. Don't think I didn't notice.

FRANK. Millie, darling! Really! I detest the woman.

MILLIE. Then what were you doing in her box at Lord's?

FRANK. Carstairs invited me. I went there because it was a good place to see the match from.

MILLIE. Yes, I'm sure it was. Much better than the grandstand, anyway.

FRANK (*remembering something suddenly*). Oh, my God!

MILLIE (*coming below the desk*). It's all right, my dear. Don't bother to apologize. We gave the seat away, as it happens.

FRANK. I'm most terribly sorry.

MILLIE. It's all right. (*She moves to* R. *of the desk.*) We couldn't afford a box, you see.

FRANK (*moving a few steps towards* R.C.). It wasn't that. You know it wasn't that. It's just that I—well, I clean forgot.

MILLIE. Funny you didn't forget the Carstairs invitation.

FRANK. Millie—don't be a fool.

MILLIE. It's you who are the fool. (*Appealingly.*) Frank—have you never been in love? I know you're not in love with me—but haven't you ever been in love with anyone? Don't you realize what torture you inflict on someone who loves you when you do a thing like that?

FRANK. I've told you I'm sorry—I don't know what more I can say.

MILLIE. Why not the truth?

FRANK. The truth is—I clean forgot.

MILLIE. The truth is—you had something better to do—and why not say it?

FRANK. All right. Believe that if you like. It happens to be a lie, but believe it all the same. Only for God's sake stop this. (*He turns and moves down* R.)

MILLIE. Then for God's sake show me some pity. Do you think it's any pleasanter for me to believe that you cut me because you forgot? Do you think that doesn't hurt either?

(FRANK *turns away.*)

(*She moves above the up* R. *corner of the desk and faces the door up* L.) Oh damn! I was so determined to be brave and not mention Lord's. Why did I? Frank, just tell me one thing. Just tell me you're not running away from me—that's all I want to hear.

FRANK. I'm coming to Bradford.

MILLIE (*turning to* FRANK). I think, if you don't, I'll kill myself.

FRANK (*turning and taking a few steps in towards* MILLIE). I'm coming to Bradford.

(*The door up* R. *opens.* FRANK *stops at the sound.* MILLIE *recovers herself and crosses above the table* C. *to the sideboard.* ANDREW CROCKER-HARRIS *enters and appears from behind the screen. Despite the summer sun he wears a serge suit and a stiff collar. He carries a mackintosh and a rolled-up time-table and looks, as ever, neat, complacent and unruffled. He speaks in a very gentle voice which he rarely raises.*)

ANDREW (*hanging his mackintosh on the hall-stand*). Is Taplow here?

(FRANK *eases towards the fireplace.*)

MILLIE. I sent him to the chemist to get your prescription made up.

ANDREW. What prescription?

MILLIE. Your heart medicine. Don't you remember? You told me this morning it had run out.

ANDREW. Of course I remember, my dear, but there was no need to send Taplow for it. If you had telephoned the chemist he would have sent it round in plenty of time. He knows the prescription. (*He comes down to the* L. *end of the settee.*) Now Taplow will be late and I am so pressed for time I hardly know how to fit him in. (*He sees* FRANK.) Ah, Hunter! How are you? (*He moves* R. *to* FRANK.)

FRANK. Very well, thanks.

(*They shake hands.*)

ANDREW. Most kind of you to drop in, but, as Millie should have warned you, I am expecting a pupil for extra work and . . .

MILLIE. He's staying to dinner, Andrew.

ANDREW. Good. Then I shall see something of you. However, when Taplow returns I'm sure you won't mind . . .

FRANK (*making a move*). No, of course not. I'll make myself scarce now, if you'd rather—I mean, if you're busy . . .

(*He turns away and moves* C.)

ANDREW. Oh no. There is no need for that. Sit down, do. Will you smoke? I don't, as you know, but Millie does. (*He crosses below the desk and moves up* L. *of it.*) Millie, give our guest a cigarette.

MILLIE (*moving down to the table* C.). I haven't any, I'm afraid. I've had to cadge from him. (*She takes a copy of the "Tatler" from the basket.*)

(ANDREW *opens the drawer that should contain the scissors.* FRANK *takes out his cigarette case, crosses to* R. *of the table* C., *and offers it to* MILLIE. *She exchanges a glance with him as she takes a cigarette.*)

ANDREW (*looking for the scissors*). We expected you at Lord's, Hunter.

FRANK. What? Oh yes. I'm most terribly sorry. I . . .

MILLIE (*crossing behind the settee*). He clean forgot, Andrew. Imagine.

ANDREW. Forgot?

MILLIE. Not everyone is blessed with your superhuman memory, you see.

FRANK. I really can't apologize enough.

ANDREW. Please don't bother to mention it. On the second day we managed to sell the seat to a certain Dr Lambert, who wore, I regret to say, the colours of the opposing faction, but who otherwise seemed a passably agreeable person. (*He moves above the table* C.) You liked him, didn't you, Millie?

MILLIE (*looking at* FRANK.) Very much indeed. I thought him quite charming.

ANDREW. A charming old gentleman. (*To* FRANK.) You have had tea? (*He picks up the scissors.*)

FRANK. Yes—thank you.

ANDREW. Is there any other refreshment I can offer you?

FRANK. No, thank you.

ANDREW (*cutting the string round the time-table*). Would it interest you to see the new time-table I have drafted for next term?

FRANK. Yes, very much. (*He moves up* R. *of* ANDREW.)

(ANDREW *opens out a long roll of paper, made by pasting pieces of foolscap together, and which is entirely covered by his meticulous writing.*)

FRANK. I never knew you drafted our time-tables.

ANDREW. Didn't you? I have done so for the last fifteen years.

(MILLIE *wanders down* R. *of the settee.*)

Of course, they are always issued in mimeograph under the headmaster's signature. Now what form do you take? Upper fifth Science—there you are—that's the general picture; but on the back you will see each form specified under separate headings—there—that's a new idea of mine—Millie, this might interest you.

MILLIE (*sitting in the easy chair; suddenly harsh*). You know it bores me to death.

(FRANK *looks up, surprised and uncomfortable.* ANDREW *does not remove his eyes from the time-table.*)

ANDREW. Millie has no head for this sort of work. There you see. Now here you can follow the upper fifth Science throughout every day of the week.

FRANK (*indicating the time-table.*) I must say, I think this is a really wonderful job.

ANDREW. Thank you. It has the merit of clarity, I think. (*He starts to roll up the time-table.*)

FRANK. I don't know what they'll do without you.

ANDREW (*without expression*). They'll find somebody else, I expect.

(*There is a pause.*)

FRANK. What sort of job is this you're going to?

ANDREW (*looking at* MILLIE *for the first time*). Hasn't Millie told you?

FRANK. She said it was a cr—— a private school.

ANDREW. A crammer's—for backward boys. It is run by an old Oxford contemporary of mine who lives in Dorset. (*He moves round* L *of the table* C. *and finishes rolling up the time-table.*) The work will not be so arduous as here and my doctor seems to think I will be able to undertake it without—er danger.

FRANK (*with genuine sympathy*). It's the most rotten bad luck for you. I'm awfully sorry.

ANDREW (*raising his voice a little*). My dear Hunter, there is nothing whatever to be sorry for. I am looking forward to the change.

(*There is a knock at the door up* R.)

Come in. (*He crosses below the table to* C.)

(TAPLOW *enters up* R., *a trifle breathless and guilty-looking. He carries a medicine bottle wrapped and sealed.*)

Ah, Taplow. Good. You have been running, I see.

TAPLOW. Yes, sir. (*He crosses to the* L. *end of the settee.*)

ANDREW. There was a queue at the chemist's, I suppose?

TAPLOW. Yes, sir.

ANDREW. And doubtless an even longer one at Stewart's?

TAPLOW. Yes, sir—I mean—no, sir—I mean—

(*he looks at* MILLIE) yes, sir. (*He crosses below the settee to* MILLIE *and hands her the medicine.*)

MILLIE. You were late yourself, Andrew.

ANDREW. Exactly. And for that I apologize, Taplow.

TAPLOW. That's all right, sir.

ANDREW (*crossing below the desk and moving* L. *of it*). Luckily we have still a good hour before lock-up, so nothing has been lost. (*He puts the time-table on the desk.*)

FRANK (*moving to the door up* L. ; *to* MILLIE). May I use the short cut? I'm going back to my digs.

(ANDREW *sits at his desk and opens a book.*)

MILLIE (*rising and moving up* R. *of the settee*). Yes. Go ahead. Come back soon. If Andrew hasn't finished we can sit in the garden. (*She crosses above the table* C. *and picks up the shopping basket. She puts the medicine on the sideboard.*) I'd better go and see about dinner.

(*She goes out up* C.)

ANDREW (*to* FRANK). Taplow is desirous of obtaining a remove from my form, Hunter, so that he can spend the rest of his career here playing happily with the crucibles, retorts and bunsen burners of your science fifth.

FRANK (*turning at the door*). Oh. Has he?

ANDREW. Has he what?

FRANK. Obtained his remove?

ANDREW (*after a pause*). He has obtained exactly what he deserves. No less; and certainly no more.

(TAPLOW *mutters an explosion of mirth.* FRANK *nods, thoughtfully, and goes out.* ANDREW *has caught sight of* TAPLOW'S *contorted face, but passes no remark on it. He beckons* TAPLOW *across and signs to him to sit in the chair* R. *of the desk.* TAPLOW *sits.* ANDREW *picks up a copy of* "*The Agamemnon*" *and* TAPLOW *does the same.*)

ANDREW. Line thirteen hundred and ninety-nine. Begin. (*He leans back.*)

TAPLOW (*reading slowly*). Chorus. We—are surprised at . . .

ANDREW (*automatically*). We marvel at.

TAPLOW. We marvel at—thy tongue—how bold thou art—that you . . .

ANDREW. Thou. (*His interruptions are automatic. His thoughts are evidently far distant.*)

TAPLOW. Thou—can . . .

ANDREW. Canst.

TAPLOW. Canst—boastfully speak . . .

ANDREW. Utter such a boastful speech.

TAPLOW. Utter such a boastful speech—over—(*in a sudden rush of inspiration*) the bloody corpse of the husband you have slain.

(ANDREW *puts on his glasses and looks down at his text for the first time.* TAPLOW *looks apprehensive.*)

ANDREW (*after a pause*). Taplow—I presume you are using a different text from mine.

TAPLOW. No, sir.

ANDREW. That is strange, for the line as I have it reads: " *ἥτις τοιόνδ' ἐπ' ἀνδρὶ κομπάζεις λόγον.*"* However diligently I search I can discover no " bloody "—no " corpse "—no " you have slain." Simply " husband ".

TAPLOW. Yes, sir. That's right.

ANDREW. Then why do you invent words that simply are not there?

TAPLOW. I thought they sounded better, sir. More exciting. After all, she did kill her husband, sir. (*With relish.*) She's just been revealed with his dead body and Cassandra's weltering in gore.

ANDREW. I am delighted at this evidence, Taplow, of your interest in the rather more lurid aspects of dramaturgy, but I feel I must remind you that you are supposed to be construing Greek, not collaborating with Aeschylus. (*He leans back.*)

* *Phonetically represented, this reads:* " heetis toiond ep andri compadzise logon."

TAPLOW (*greatly daring*). Yes, but still, sir, translator's licence, sir—I didn't get anything wrong—and after all it *is* a play and not just a bit of Greek construe.

ANDREW (*momentarily at a loss*). I seem to detect a note of end of term in your remarks. I am not denying that *The Agamemnon* is a play. It is perhaps the greatest play ever written. (*He leans forward.*)

TAPLOW (*quickly*). I wonder how many people in the form think that? (*He pauses; instantly frightened of what he has said.*) Sorry, sir. Shall I go on?

(ANDREW *does not answer. He sits motionless, staring at his book.*)

Shall I go on, sir?

(*There is another pause.* ANDREW *raises his head slowly from his book.*)

ANDREW (*murmuring gently, not looking at* TAPLOW). When I was a very young man, only two years older than you are now, Taplow, I wrote, for my own pleasure, a translation of *The Agamemnon*—a very free translation—I remember—in rhyming couplets.

TAPLOW. The whole *Agamemnon*—in verse? That must have been hard work, sir.

ANDREW. It was hard work; but I derived great joy from it. The play had so excited and moved me that I wished to communicate, however imperfectly, some of that emotion to others. When I had finished it, I remember, I thought it very beautiful—almost more beautiful than the original. (*He leans back.*)

TAPLOW. Was it ever published, sir?

ANDREW. No. Yesterday I looked for the manuscript while I was packing my papers. I was unable to find it. I fear it is lost—like so many other things. Lost for good.

TAPLOW. Hard luck, sir.

(ANDREW *is silent again.* TAPLOW *steals a timid glance at him.*)

Shall I go on, sir?

(ANDREW, *with a slight effort, lowers his eyes again to his text.*)

ANDREW (*leaning forward; raising his voice slightly*). No. Go back and get that last line right.

(TAPLOW, *out of* ANDREW'S *vision, as he thinks, makes a disgusted grimace in his direction.*)

TAPLOW. That—thou canst utter such a boastful speech over thy husband.

ANDREW. Yes. And now, if you would be so kind, you will do the line again, without the facial contortion which you just found necessary to accompany it.

(TAPLOW *is about to begin the line again.* MILLIE *enters up* C., *hurriedly. She is wearing an apron.* TAPLOW *rises.*)

MILLIE. The headmaster's just coming up the drive. Don't tell him I'm in. The fish pie isn't in the oven yet.

(*She exits up* C.)

TAPLOW (*turning hopefully to* ANDREW). I'd better go, hadn't I, sir? I mean—I don't want to be in the way.

ANDREW. We do not yet know that it is I the headmaster wishes to see. Other people live in this building.

(*There is a knock at the door up* R.)

Come in.

(DR FROBISHER *enters up* R. *He looks more like a distinguished diplomat than a doctor of literature and a classical scholar. He is in the middle fifties and goes to a very good tailor.* ANDREW *rises.*)

FROBISHER. Ah, Crocker-Harris, I've caught you in. I'm so glad. (*He crosses behind the settee and comes down* L. *of it.*) I hope I'm not disturbing you?

ANDREW. I have been taking a pupil in extra work.

(TAPLOW *eases below the table* C.)

FROBISHER. On the penultimate day of term? That argues either great conscientiousness on your part or considerable backwardness on his.

ANDREW. Perhaps a combination of both.

FROBISHER. Quite so, but as this is my only chance of speaking to you before tomorrow, I think that perhaps your pupil will be good enough to excuse us. (*He turns politely to* TAPLOW.)

TAPLOW. Oh yes, sir. That's really quite all right. (*He grabs his books off* ANDREW'S *desk.*)

ANDREW (*crossing to* TAPLOW). I'm extremely sorry, Taplow. You will please explain to your father exactly what occurred over this lost hour and tell him that I shall in due course be writing to him to return the money involved.

(FROBISHER *moves below the settee to the fireplace.*)

TAPLOW (*hurriedly*). Yes, sir. But please don't bother, sir. (*He dashes to the door up* R.) I know it's all right, sir. Thank you, sir.

(*He darts out.*)

FROBISHER (*idly picking up an ornament on the mantelpiece*). Have the Gilberts called on you yet? (*He turns to* ANDREW.)

ANDREW (*moving* C.). The Gilberts, sir? Who are they?

FROBISHER. Gilbert is your successor with the lower fifth. He is down here today with his wife, and as they will be taking over this flat I thought perhaps you wouldn't mind if they came in to look it over.

ANDREW. Of course not.

FROBISHER. I've told you about him, I think. He is a very brilliant young man and won exceptionally high honours at Oxford.

ANDREW. So I understand, sir.

FROBISHER. Not, of course, as high as the honours you yourself won there. He didn't, for instance, win the Chancellor's prize for Latin verse or the Gainsford.

ANDREW. He won the Hertford Latin, then?

FROBISHER (*replacing the ornament*). No. (*Mildly surprised.*) Did you win that, too?

(ANDREW *nods.*)

It's sometimes rather hard to remember that you are perhaps the most brilliant classical scholar we have ever had at the school.

ANDREW. You are very kind.

FROBISHER (*urbanely correcting his gaffe*). Hard to remember, I mean—because of your other activities—your brilliant work on the school time-table, for instance, and also for your heroic battle for so long and against such odds with the soul-destroying lower fifth.

ANDREW. I have not found that my soul has been destroyed by the lower fifth, Headmaster.

FROBISHER. I was joking, of course.

ANDREW. Oh. I see.

FROBISHER. Is your wife in?

ANDREW. Er—no. Not at the moment.

FROBISHER. I shall have a chance of saying good-bye to her tomorrow. (*He moves in a few steps below the settee.*) I am rather glad I have got you to myself. I have a delicate matter—two rather delicate matters—to broach.

ANDREW (*moving in slightly; indicating the settee*). Please sit down. (*He stands at the* L. *end of the settee.*)

FROBISHER. Thank you. (*He sits.*) Now you have been with us, in all, eighteen years, haven't you?

(ANDREW *nods.*)

It is extremely unlucky that you should have had to retire at so comparatively an early age and so short a time before you would have been eligible for a pension. (*He is regarding his nails, as he speaks, studiously avoiding meeting* ANDREW's *gaze.*)

(ANDREW *crosses below the settee to the fireplace and stands facing it.*)

ANDREW (*after a pause*). You have decided, then, not to award me a pension?

FROBISHER. Not I, my dear fellow. It has nothing at all to do with me. It's the governors who, I'm afraid, have been forced to turn down your application. I put your case to them as well as I could——

(ANDREW *turns and faces* FROBISHER.)

—but they decided with great regret, that they couldn't make an exception to the rule.

ANDREW. But I thought—my wife thought, that an exception was made some five years ago . . .

FROBISHER. Ah! In the case of Buller, you mean? True. But the circumstances with Buller were quite remarkable. It was, after all, in playing rugger against the school that he received that injury.

ANDREW. Yes. I remember.

FROBISHER. And then the governors received a petition from boys, old boys and parents, with over five hundred signatures.

ANDREW. I would have signed that petition myself, but through some oversight I was not asked.

FROBISHER. He was a splendid fellow, Buller. Splendid. Doing very well, too, now, I gather.

ANDREW. I'm delighted to hear it.

FROBISHER. Your own case, of course, is equally deserving. If not more so—for Buller was a younger man. Unfortunately—rules are rules—and are not made to be broken every few years; at any rate that is the governors' view.

ANDREW. I quite understand.

FROBISHER. I knew you would. Now might I ask you a rather impertinent question?

ANDREW. Certainly.

FROBISHER. You have, I take it, private means?

ANDREW. My wife has some.

FROBISHER. Ah, yes. Your wife has often told me of her family connexions. I understand her father has a business in—Bradford—isn't it?

ANDREW. Yes. He runs a men's clothing shop in the Arcade.

FROBISHER. Indeed? Your wife's remarks had led me to imagine something a little more—extensive.

ANDREW. My father-in-law made a settlement on my wife at the time of our marriage. She has about three hundred a year of her own. I have nothing. Is that the answer to your question, Headmaster?

FROBISHER. Yes. Thank you for your frankness. Now, this private school you are going to . . .

ANDREW. My salary at the crammer's is to be two hundred pounds a year.

FROBISHER. Quite so. With board and lodging, of course?

ANDREW. For eight months of the year.

FROBISHER. Yes, I see. (*He ponders a second.*) Of course, you know, there is the School Benevolent Fund that deals with cases of actual hardship.

ANDREW. There will be no actual hardship, Headmaster.

FROBISHER. No. I am glad you take that view. I must admit, though, I had hoped that your own means had proved a little more ample. Your wife had certainly led me to suppose . . .

ANDREW. I am not denying that a pension would have been very welcome, Headmaster, but I see no reason to quarrel with the governors' decision. What is the other delicate matter you have to discuss?

FROBISHER. Well, it concerns the arrangements at prize-giving tomorrow. You are, of course, prepared to say a few words?

ANDREW. I had assumed you would call on me to do so.

FROBISHER. Of course. It is always done, and I know the boys appreciate the custom.

ANDREW (*crossing to the upstage end of the desk*). I have already made a few notes of what I am going to say. Perhaps you would care . . .

FROBISHER. No, no. That isn't necessary at all. I know I can trust your discretion—not to say your wit. It will be, I know, a very moving moment for you—indeed for us all—but, as I'm sure you realize, it is far better to keep these occasions from becoming too heavy and distressing. You know how little the boys appreciate sentiment.

ANDREW. I do.

FROBISHER. That is why I've planned my own reference to you at the end of my speech to be rather more light and jocular than I would otherwise have made it.

ANDREW. I quite understand. (*He moves to* L. *of the desk, puts on his glasses and picks up his speech.*) I too have prepared a few little jokes and puns for my speech. One—a play of words on *vale*, farewell and Wally, the Christian name of a backward boy in my class, is, I think, rather happy.

FROBISHER. Yes. (*He laughs belatedly.*) Very neat. That should go down extremely well.

ANDREW. I'm glad you like it.

FROBISHER (*rising and crossing to* R. *of the desk*). Well, now—there is a particular favour I have to ask of you in connexion with the ceremony, and I know I shall not have to ask in vain. Fletcher, as you know, is leaving too.

ANDREW. Yes. He is going into the city, they tell me.

FROBISHER. Yes. Now he is, of course, considerably junior to you. He has only been here—let me see—five years. But, as you know, he has done great things for our cricket—positive wonders, when you remember what doldrums we were in before he came.

ANDREW. Our win at Lord's this year was certainly most inspiriting.

FROBISHER. Exactly. (*He moves above the desk.*) Now I'm sure that tomorrow the boys will make the occasion of his farewell speech a tremendous demonstration of gratitude. The applause might go on for minutes—you know what the boys feel about Lord's—and I seriously doubt my ability to cut it short or even, I admit, the propriety of trying to do so. Now, you see the quandary in which I am placed?

ANDREW. Perfectly. You wish to refer to me and for me to make my speech before you come to Fletcher?

FROBISHER. It's extremely awkward, and I feel wretched about asking it of you—but it's more for your own sake than for mine or Fletcher's that I do. After all, a climax is what one must try to work up to on these occasions.

ANDREW. Naturally, Headmaster, I wouldn't wish to provide an anti-climax.

FROBISHER. You really mustn't take it amiss, my dear fellow. The boys, in applauding Fletcher for several minutes and yourself say—for—well, for not quite so long—won't be making any personal demonstration between you. It will be quite impersonal—I assure you—quite impersonal.

ANDREW. I understand.

FROBISHER (*patting* ANDREW'S *shoulder; warmly*). I knew you would (*he looks at his watch*) and I can hardly tell you how wisely I think you have chosen. Well now—as that is all my business, I think perhaps I had better be getting along. (*He crosses to* R. *of the table* C.) This has been a terribly busy day for me—for you too, I imagine.

ANDREW. Yes.

(MILLIE *enters up* C. *She has taken off her apron, and tidied herself up. She comes to* L. *of* FROBISHER.)

MILLIE (*in her social manner*). Ah, Headmaster. How good of you to drop in.

FROBISHER (*more at home with her than with* ANDREW). Mrs Crocker-Harris. How are you?

(*They shake hands.*)

You're looking extremely well, I must say. (*To* ANDREW.) Has anyone ever told you, Crocker-Harris, that you have a very attractive wife?

ANDREW. Many people, sir. But then I hardly need to be told.

MILLIE. Can I persuade you to stay a few moments and have a drink, Headmaster? It's so rarely we have the pleasure of seeing you.

FROBISHER. Unfortunately, dear lady, I was just on the point of leaving. I have two frantic parents waiting for me at home. You are dining with us tomorrow—both of you, aren't you?

MILLIE. Yes, indeed—and so looking forward to it.

(FROBISHER *and* MILLIE *move to the door up* R.)

FROBISHER. I'm so glad. We can say our sad farewells then. (*To* ANDREW.) Au revoir, Crocker-Harris, and thank you very much. (*He opens the door.*)

(ANDREW *gives a slight bow.* MILLIE *holds the door open.* FROBISHER *goes out.*)

MILLIE (*to* ANDREW). Don't forget to take your medicine, dear, will you?

(*She goes out.*)

ANDREW. No.

FROBISHER (*off*). Lucky invalid! To have such a very charming nurse.

MILLIE (*off*). I really don't know what to say to all these compliments, Headmaster. I don't believe you mean a word of them.

(ANDREW *turns and looks out of the window.*)

FROBISHER (*off*). Every word. Till tomorrow, then? Good-bye.

(*The outer door is heard to slam.* ANDREW *is staring out of the window.* MILLIE *enters up* R.)

MILLIE. Well? Do we get it? (*She stands on the step.*)

ANDREW (*turning and moving below the chair* L. *of his desk; absently*). Get what?

MILLIE. The pension, of course. Do we get it?

ANDREW. No.

MILLIE (*crossing above the settee to* C.). My God! Why not?

ANDREW (*sitting at his desk*). It's against the rules.

MILLIE. Buller got it, didn't he? Buller got it? What's the idea of giving it to him and not to us?

ANDREW. The governors are afraid of establishing a precedent.

MILLIE. The mean old brutes! My God, what I wouldn't like to say to them! (*She moves above the desk and rounds on* ANDREW.) And what did you say? Just sat there and made a joke in Latin, I suppose?

ANDREW. There wasn't very much I could say, in Latin or any other language.

MILLIE. Oh, wasn't there? I'd have said it all right. I wouldn't just have sat there twiddling my thumbs and taking it from that old phoney of a headmaster. But, then, of course, I'm not a man.

(ANDREW *is turning the pages of* " *The Agamemnon* ", *not looking at her.*)

What do they expect you to do? Live on my money, I suppose.

ANDREW. There has never been any question of that. I shall be perfectly able to support myself.

MILLIE. Yourself? Doesn't the marriage service say something about the husband supporting his wife? (*She leans on the desk.*) Doesn't it? You ought to know.

ANDREW. Yes, it does.

MILLIE. And how do you think you're going to do that on two hundred a year?

ANDREW. I shall do my utmost to save some of it. You're welcome to it, if I can.

MILLIE. Thank you for precisely nothing.

(ANDREW *underlines a word in the text he is reading.*)

What else did the old fool have to say? (*She moves to* R. *of the chair,* R. *of the desk.*)

ANDREW. The headmaster? He wants me to make my speech tomorrow before instead of after Fletcher.

MILLIE (*sitting* R. *of the desk*). Yes. I knew he was going to ask that.

ANDREW (*without surprise*). You knew?

MILLIE. Yes. He asked my advice about it a week ago. I told him to go ahead. I knew you wouldn't mind, and as there isn't a Mrs Fletcher to make *me* look a fool, I didn't give two hoots.

(*There is a knock on the door up* R.)

Come in.

(MR *and* MRS GILBERT *enter up* R. *He is about twenty-two, and his wife a year or so younger.* MILLIE *rises and stands at the downstage corner of the desk.*)

GILBERT. Mr Crocker-Harris?

ANDREW. Yes. (*He rises.*) Is it Mr and Mrs Gilbert? The headmaster told me you might look in.

MRS GILBERT (*crossing above the settee to* C.). I do hope we're not disturbing you.

(GILBERT *follows* MRS GILBERT *and stands down stage of, and slightly behind, her.*)

ANDREW. Not at all. This is my wife.

MRS GILBERT. How do you do?

ANDREW. Mr and Mrs Gilbert are our successors to this flat, my dear.

MILLIE. Oh yes. (*She moves to* L. *of* MRS GILBERT.) How nice to meet you both.

GILBERT. How do you do? We really won't

keep you more than a second—my wife thought as we were here you wouldn't mind us taking a squint at our future home.

MRS GILBERT (*unnecessarily*). This is the drawing-room, I suppose?

(GILBERT *crosses to the fireplace. He looks for a moment at the picture above the mantelpiece, then turns and watches the others.*)

MILLIE. Well, it's really a living-room. Andrew uses it as a study.

MRS GILBERT. How charmingly you've done it!

MILLIE. Oh, do you think so? I'm afraid it isn't nearly as nice as I'd like to make it—but a schoolmaster's wife has to think of so many other things besides curtains and covers. Boys with dirty books and a husband with leaky fountain pens, for instance.

MRS GILBERT. Yes, I suppose so. Of course, I haven't been a schoolmaster's wife for very long, you know.

GILBERT. Don't swank, darling. You haven't been a schoolmaster's wife at all yet.

MRS GILBERT. Oh yes, I have—for two months. You were a schoolmaster when I married you.

GILBERT. Prep school doesn't count.

MILLIE. Have you only been married two months?

MRS GILBERT. Two months and sixteen days.

GILBERT. Seventeen.

MILLIE (*sentimentally*). Andrew, did you hear? They've only been married two months.

ANDREW. Indeed? Is that all?

MRS GILBERT (*crossing above* MILLIE *to the window*). Oh, look, darling. They've got a garden. It is yours, isn't it?

MILLIE. Oh, yes. It's only a pocket handkerchief, I'm afraid, but it's very useful to Andrew. He often works out there, don't you, dear?

ANDREW. Yes, indeed. I find it very agreeable.

MILLIE (*moving to the door up* C.). Shall I show you

the rest of the flat? It's a bit untidy, I'm afraid, but you must forgive that. (*She opens the door.*)

MRS GILBERT (*moving up to* L. *of* MILLIE). Oh, of course.

MILLIE. And the kitchen is in a terrible mess. I'm in the middle of cooking dinner.

MRS GILBERT (*breathlessly*). Oh, do you cook?

MILLIE. Oh, yes. I have to. We haven't had a maid for five years.

MRS GILBERT. Oh! I do think that's wonderful of you. I'm scared stiff of having to do it for Peter—I know the first dinner I have to cook for him will wreck our married life.

GILBERT. Highly probable.

(MRS GILBERT *exits up* C.)

MILLIE (*following* MRS GILBERT). Well, these days we've all got to try and do things we weren't really brought up to do.

(*She goes out, closing the door.*)

ANDREW (*to* GILBERT). Don't you want to see the rest of the flat?

GILBERT (*crossing to* C.). No. I leave all that sort of thing to my wife. She's the boss. I thought perhaps you could tell me something about the lower fifth.

ANDREW. What would you like to know?

GILBERT. Well, sir, quite frankly, I'm petrified.

ANDREW. I don't think you need to be. May I give you some sherry? (*He comes down* L. *to the cupboard.*)

GILBERT. Thank you.

ANDREW. They are mostly boys of about fifteen or sixteen. They are not very difficult to handle. (*He takes out a bottle and a glass.*)

GILBERT. The headmaster said you ruled them with a rod of iron. He called you "the Himmler of the lower fifth."

ANDREW (*turning, bottle and glass in hand*). Did he? "The Himmler of the lower fifth." I think he exaggerated. I hope he exaggerated. " The Himmler of the lower fifth." (*He puts the bottle on the desk, then fills the glass.*)

GILBERT (*puzzled*). He only meant that you kept the most wonderful discipline. I must say I do admire you for that. I couldn't even manage that with eleven-year-olds, so what I'll be like with fifteens and sixteens I shudder to think. (*He moves below the chair* R. *of the desk.*)

ANDREW. It is not so difficult. (*He hands* GILBERT *the glass.*) They aren't bad boys. Sometimes a little wild and unfeeling, perhaps—but not bad. " The Himmler of the lower fifth." Dear me! (*He turns to the cabinet with the bottle.*)

GILBERT. Perhaps I shouldn't have said that. I've been tactless, I'm afraid.

ANDREW. Oh no. (*He puts the bottle in the cupboard.*) Please sit down. (*He stands by the downstage end of the desk.*)

GILBERT. Thank you, sir. (*He sits* R. *of the desk.*)

ANDREW. From the very beginning I realized that I didn't possess the knack of making myself liked—a knack that you will find you do possess.

GILBERT. Do you think so?

ANDREW. Oh yes. I am quite sure of it. (*He moves up* L. *of the desk.*) It is not a quality of great importance to a schoolmaster though, for too much of it, as you may also find, is as great a danger as the total lack of it. Forgive me lecturing, won't you?

GILBERT. I want to learn.

ANDREW. I can only teach you from my own experience. For two or three years I tried very hard to communicate to the boys some of my own joy in the great literature of the past. Of course I failed, as you will fail, nine hundred and ninety-nine times out of a thousand. But a single success can atone, and more than atone, for all the failures in the world. And sometimes—very rarely, it is true—but sometimes I had that success. That was in the early years.

GILBERT (*eagerly listening*). Please go on, sir.

ANDREW. In early years too, I discovered an easy substitute for popularity. (*He picks up his speech.*) I had of course acquired—we all do—many little mannerisms and tricks of speech, and I found that the boys were beginning to laugh at me. I was very happy at that, and encouraged the boys' laughter by playing up to it. It made our relationship so very much easier. They didn't like me as a man, but they found me funny as a character, and you can teach more things by laughter than by earnestness—for I never did have much sense of humour. So, for a time, you see, I was quite a success as a schoolmaster . . . (*He stops.*) I fear this is all very personal and embarrassing to you. Forgive me. You need have no fears about the lower fifth. (*He puts the speech into his pocket and turns to the window.*)

(GILBERT *rises and moves above the desk.*)

GILBERT (*after a pause*). I'm afraid I said something that hurt you very much. It's myself you must forgive, sir. Believe me, I'm desperately sorry.

ANDREW (*turning down stage and leaning slightly on the back of the swivel chair*). There's no need. You were merely telling me what I should have known for myself. Perhaps I did in my heart, and hadn't the courage to acknowledge it. I knew, of course, that I was not only not liked, but now positively disliked. I had realized too that the boys—for many long years now—had ceased to laugh at me. I don't know why they no longer found me a joke. Perhaps it was my illness. No, I don't think it was that. Something deeper than that. Not a sickness of the body, but a sickness of the soul. At all events it didn't take much discernment on my part to realize I had become an utter failure as a schoolmaster. Still, stupidly enough, I hadn't realized that I was also feared. "The Himmler of the lower fifth." I suppose that will become my epitaph.

(GILBERT *is now deeply embarrassed and rather upset, but he remains silent.*)

(*He sits on the upstage end of the window seat. With a mild laugh.*) I cannot for the life of me imagine why I should choose to unburden myself to you—a total stranger—when I have been silent to others for so long. Perhaps it is because my very unworthy mantle is about to fall on your shoulders. If that is so I shall take a prophet's privilege and foretell that you will have a very great success with the lower fifth.

GILBERT. Thank you, sir. I shall do my best.

ANDREW. I can't offer you a cigarette, I'm afraid. I don't smoke.

GILBERT. That's all right, sir. Nor do I.

MRS GILBERT (*off*). Thank you so much for showing me round.

(MILLIE *and* MRS GILBERT *enter up* C. ANDREW *rises.* MILLIE *comes down* R. *of the table* C., *picks up the papers on the settee and puts them on the fender down* R. MRS GILBERT *comes down* L. *of the table* C. *to* R. *of* GILBERT.)

ANDREW. I trust your wife has found no major snags in your new flat.

MRS GILBERT. No. None at all.

MRS GILBERT. Just imagine, Peter. Mr and Mrs Crocker-Harris first met each other on a holiday in the Lake District. Isn't that a coincidence?

GILBERT (*a little distrait*). Yes. Yes, it certainly is. On a walking tour, too?

(ANDREW *turns and looks out of the window.*)

MILLIE. Andrew was on a walking tour. No walking for me. I can't abide it. I was staying with my uncle—that's Sir William Bartop, you know—you may have heard of him.

(GILBERT *and* MRS GILBERT *try to look as though they had heard of him constantly.*)

(*She moves below the settee.*) He'd taken a house near Windermere—quite a mansion it was really—rather silly for an old gentleman living alone—and Andrew knocked on our front door one day and asked the footman for a glass of water. So my uncle invited him in to tea.

MRS GILBERT (*moving* C.). Our meeting wasn't quite as romantic as that.

GILBERT. I knocked her flat on her face. (*He moves behind* MRS GILBERT *and puts his hands on her shoulders.*)

MRS GILBERT. Not with love at first sight. With the swing doors of our hotel bar. So of course then he apologized and . . .

(ANDREW *turns and faces into the room.*)

GILBERT (*brusquely*). Darling. The Crocker-Harris's, I'm sure, have far more important things to do than to listen to your detailed but inaccurate account of our very sordid little encounter. Why not just say I married you for your money and leave it at that? Come on, we must go.

MRS GILBERT (*moving above the settee ; to* MILLIE). Isn't he awful to me?

MILLIE (*moving round the* R. *end of the settee to the door up* R.). Men have no souls, my dear. My husband is just as bad.

MRS GILBERT. Good-bye, Mr Crocker-Harris.

ANDREW (*with a slight bow*). Good-bye.

MRS GILBERT (*moving to the door up* R. ; *to* MILLIE). I think your idea about the dining-room is awfully good—if only I can get the permit . . .

(MILLIE *and* MRS GILBERT *go out.* GILBERT *has dallied to say good-bye alone to* ANDREW.)

GILBERT. Good-bye, sir.

ANDREW (*crossing* C. *to* L. *of* GILBERT). Er—you will, I know, respect the confidences I have just made to you.

GILBERT. I should hate you to think I wouldn't.

ANDREW. I am sorry to have embarrassed you.

I don't know what came over me. I have not been very well, you know. Good-bye, my dear fellow, and my best wishes.

GILBERT. Thank you. The very best of good luck to you too, sir, in your future career.

ANDREW. My future career? Yes. Thank you.

GILBERT. Well, good-bye, sir.

(*He crosses up* R. *and goes out.* ANDREW *moves to the chair* R. *of the desk and sits. He picks up a book and looks idly at it.* MILLIE *enters up* R. *She crosses above the table* C., *picks up the box of chocolates and eats one as she speaks.*)

MILLIE. Good-looking couple.

ANDREW. Very.

MILLIE. He looks as if he'd got what it takes. I should think he'll be a success all right.

ANDREW. That's what I thought.

MILLIE. I don't think it's much of a career, though —a schoolmaster—for a likely young chap like that.

ANDREW. I know you don't.

MILLIE (*crossing down to the desk and picking up the luggage labels*). Still, I bet when he leaves this place it won't be without a pension. It'll be roses, roses all the way, and tears and cheers and good-bye, Mr Chips.

ANDREW. I expect so.

MILLIE. What's the matter with you?

ANDREW. Nothing.

MILLIE. You're not going to have another of your attacks, are you? You look dreadful.

ANDREW. I'm perfectly all right.

MILLIE (*indifferently*). You know best. Your medicine's there, anyway, if you want it.

(*She goes out up* C. ANDREW, *left alone, continues for a time staring at the text he has been pretending to read. Then he puts one hand over his eyes. There is a knock on the door up* R.)

ANDREW. Come in.

(TAPLOW *enters up* R. *and appears timidly from behind the screen. He is carrying a small book behind his back.*)

(*Sharply.*) Yes, Taplow? What is it?

TAPLOW. Nothing, sir.

ANDREW. What do you mean, nothing?

TAPLOW (*timidly*). I just came back to say good-bye, sir.

ANDREW. Oh. (*He puts down the book and rises.*)

TAPLOW (*moving* C.). I didn't have a chance with the head here. I rather dashed out, I'm afraid. I thought I'd just come back and—wish you luck, sir.

ANDREW. Thank you, Taplow. That's good of you.

TAPLOW. I—er—thought this might interest you, sir. (*He quickly thrusts the small book towards* ANDREW.)

ANDREW (*taking out his glasses and putting them on*). What is it?

TAPLOW. Verse translation of *The Agamemnon*, sir. The Browning version. It's not much good. I've been reading it in the Chapel gardens.

ANDREW (*taking the book*). Very interesting, Taplow. (*He seems to have a little difficulty in speaking. He clears his throat and then goes on in his level, gentle voice.*) I know the translation, of course. It has its faults, I agree, but I think you will enjoy it more when you get used to the metre he employs. (*He hands the book to* TAPLOW.)

TAPLOW (*brusquely thrusting the book back to* ANDREW). It's for you, sir.

ANDREW. For me?

TAPLOW. Yes, sir. I've written in it.

(ANDREW *opens the fly-leaf and reads whatever is written there.*)

ANDREW. Did you buy this?

TAPLOW. Yes, sir. It was only second-hand.

ANDREW. You shouldn't have spent your pocket-money this way.

TAPLOW. That's all right, sir. It wasn't very much. (*Suddenly appalled.*) The price isn't still inside, is it?

(ANDREW *carefully wipes his glasses and puts them on again.*)

ANDREW (*at length*). No. Just what you've written. Nothing else.

TAPLOW. Good. I'm sorry you've got it already. I thought you probably would have.

ANDREW. I haven't got it already. I may have had it once. I can't remember. But I haven't got it now.

TAPLOW. That's all right, then.

(ANDREW *continues to stare at* TAPLOW'S *inscription on the fly-leaf.*)

(*Suspiciously.*) What's the matter, sir? Have I got the accent wrong on εὐμενῶς? *

ANDREW. No. The perispomenon is perfectly correct. (*His hands are shaking. He lowers the book and turns away above the chair* R. *of the desk.*) Taplow, would you be good enough to take that bottle of medicine, which you so kindly brought in, and pour me out one dose in a glass which you will find in the bathroom?

TAPLOW (*seeing something is wrong*). Yes, sir. (*He moves up to the sideboard and picks up the bottle.*)

ANDREW. The doses are clearly marked on the bottle. I usually put a little water with it.

TAPLOW. Yes, sir.

(*He darts out up* C. ANDREW, *the moment he is gone, breaks down and begins to sob uncontrollably. He sits in the chair* L. *of the desk and makes a desperate attempt, after a moment, to control himself, but when* TAPLOW *comes back his emotion is still very apparent.* TAPLOW *re-enters with the bottle and a glass, comes to the upstage end of the desk and holds out the glass.*)

**Phonetically represented, this reads :* " eumenose ".

ANDREW (*taking the glass*). Thank you. (*He drinks, turning his back on* TAPLOW *as he does so.*) You must forgive this exhibition of weakness, Taplow. The truth is I have been going through rather a strain lately.

TAPLOW (*putting the bottle on the desk*). Of course, sir. I quite understand. (*He eases towards* C.)

(*There is a knock on the door up* L.)

ANDREW. Come in.

(FRANK *enters up* L.)

FRANK. Oh, sorry. I thought you'd be finished by now. (*He moves to* L. *of* TAPLOW.)

ANDREW. Come in, Hunter, do. It's perfectly all right. Our lesson was over some time ago, but Taplow most kindly came back to say good-bye.

(FRANK, *taking in* TAPLOW's *rather startled face and* ANDREW's *obvious emotion, looks a little puzzled.*)

FRANK. Are you sure I'm not intruding?

ANDREW. No, no. I want you to see this book that Taplow has given me, Hunter. Look. A translation of *The Agamemnon*, by Robert Browning. (*He rises.*) Do you see the inscription he has put into it. (*He hands the book open to* FRANK *across the desk.*)

FRANK (*glancing at the book*). Yes, but it's no use to me, I'm afraid. I never learnt Greek.

ANDREW. Then we'll have to translate it for him, won't we, Taplow? (*He recites by heart.*) τὸν κρατοῦντα μαλθακῶς θεὸς πρόσωθεν εὐμενῶς προσδέρκεται.* That means—in a rough translation: " God from afar looks graciously upon a gentle master." It comes from a speech of Agamemnon's to Clytaemnestra.

FRANK. I see. Very pleasant and very apt. (*He hands the book back to* ANDREW.)

ANDREW. Very pleasant. But perhaps not, after all, so very apt. (*He turns quickly away from both of them as emotion once more seems about to overcome him.*)

**Phonetically rendered, this reads:* " ton kratownta malthecose theos prosothen eumenose prosdirkati."

(FRANK *brusquely jerks his head to the bewildered* TAPLOW *to get out.* TAPLOW *nods.*)

TAPLOW. Good-bye, sir, and the best of luck.
ANDREW. Good-bye, Taplow, and thank you very much.

(TAPLOW *flees quickly up* R. *and goes out.* FRANK *watches* ANDREW'S *back with a mixture of embarrassment and sympathy.*)

ANDREW (*turning at length, slightly recovered*). Dear me, what a fool I made of myself in front of that boy. And in front of you, Hunter. (*He moves in to the desk.*) I can't imagine what you must think of me.
FRANK. Nonsense.
ANDREW. I am not a very emotional person, as you know, but there was something so very touching and kindly about his action, and coming as it did just after . . . (*He stops, then glances at the book in his hand.*) This is a very delightful thing to have, don't you think?
FRANK. Delightful.
ANDREW. The quotation, of course, he didn't find entirely by himself. I happened to make some little joke about the line in form the other day. But he must have remembered it all the same to have found it so readily—and perhaps he means it.
FRANK. I'm sure he does, or he wouldn't have written it.

(MILLIE *enters up* C. *with a tray of supper things. She puts the tray on the sideboard. She puts table napkins, mats and bread on the table.* ANDREW *turns and looks out of the window.*)

MILLIE. Hullo, Frank. I'm glad you're in time. Lend me a cigarette. I've been gasping for one for an hour.

(FRANK *moves up* L. *of the table* C. *and once more extends his case.* MILLIE *takes a cigarette.*)

FRANK. Your husband has just had a very nice present.

MILLIE. Oh? Who from?

FRANK. Taplow. (*He comes down* L. *of the table.*)

MILLIE (*coming down* R. *of the table; smiling*). Oh, Taplow.

(FRANK *lights* MILLIE'S *cigarette.*)

ANDREW (*moving above the desk to the chair* R. *of it*). He bought it with his own pocket-money, Millie, and wrote a very charming inscription inside.

FRANK. "God looks kindly upon a gracious master."

ANDREW. No—not gracious—gentle, I think. τὸν κρατοῦντα μαλθακῶς—yes, I think gentle is the better translation. I would rather have had this present, I think, than almost anything I can think of.

(*There is a pause.* MILLIE *laughs suddenly.*)

MILLIE (*holding out her hand*). Let's see it. The artful little beast.

(ANDREW *hands the book across to* MILLIE. MILLIE *opens it.*)

FRANK (*urgently*). Millie.

(MILLIE *looks at* ANDREW.)

ANDREW. Artful?

(MILLIE *looks at* FRANK.)

Why artful?

(FRANK *stares meaningly at* MILLIE. MILLIE *looks at* ANDREW.)

Why artful, Millie?

(MILLIE *laughs again, quite lightly.*)

MILLIE. My dear, because I came into this room this afternoon to find him giving an imitation of you to Frank here. Obviously he was scared stiff I was going to tell you, and you'd ditch his remove or something. I don't blame him for trying a few bobs' worth of appeasement. (*She gives the book to* ANDREW, *then moves up* R. *of the table to the sideboard, where she stubs out her cigarette, picks up some cutlery and starts to lay the table.*)

(ANDREW *stands quite still, looking down at the book.*)

ANDREW (*after a pause; nodding*). I see. (*He puts the book gently on the desk, picks up the bottle of medicine and moves up* L. *of the table to the door up* C.)

MILLIE. Where are you going, dear? Dinner's nearly ready.

ANDREW (*opening the door*). Only to my room for a moment. I won't be long.

MILLIE. You've just had a dose of that, dear. I shouldn't have another, if I were you.

ANDREW. I am allowed two at a time.

MILLIE. Well, see it is two and no more, won't you?

(ANDREW *meets her eye for a moment, then goes out quietly.* MILLIE *moves to* L. *of the table and lays the last knife and fork. She looks at* FRANK *with an expression half defiant and half ashamed.*)

FRANK (*with a note of real repulsion in his voice*). Millie! My God! How could you?

MILLIE. Well, why not? (*She crosses above the table and comes down* L. *of the settee.*) Why should he be allowed his comforting little illusions? I'm not.

FRANK (*advancing on her*). Listen. You're to go to his room now and tell him that was a lie.

MILLIE. Certainly not. It wasn't a lie.

FRANK. If you don't, I will.

MILLIE. I shouldn't, if I were you. It'll only make things worse. He won't believe you.

FRANK (*moving up* R. *of the table* C.). We'll see about that.

MILLIE. Go ahead. See what happens. He

knows I don't lie to him. He knows what I told him was the truth, and he won't like your sympathy. He'll think you're making fun of him, like Taplow.

(FRANK *hesitates, then comes slowly down* C. *again.* MILLIE *watches him, a little frightened.*)

FRANK (*after a pause*). We're finished, Millie—you and I.

MILLIE (*laughing*). Frank, really! Don't be hysterical.

FRANK. I'm not. I mean it.

MILLIE (*lightly*). Oh yes, you mean it. Of course you mean it. Now just sit down, dear, and relax and forget all about artful little boys and their five bob presents, and talk to me. (*She pulls at his coat.*)

FRANK (*pulling away*). Forget? If I live to be a hundred I shall never forget that little glimpse you've just given me of yourself.

MILLIE. Frank—you're making a frightening mountain out of an absurd little molehill.

FRANK. Of course, but the mountain I'm making in my imagination is so frightening that I'd rather try to forget both it and the repulsive little molehill that gave it birth. But as I know I never can, I tell you, Millie—from this moment you and I are finished.

MILLIE (*quietly*). You can't scare me, Frank. (*She turns away towards the fireplace.*) I know that's what you're trying to do, but you can't do it.

FRANK (*quietly*). I'm not trying to scare you, Millie. I'm telling you the simple truth. I'm not coming to Bradford.

(*There is a pause.*)

MILLIE (*turning to face* FRANK; *with an attempt at bravado*). All right, my dear, if that's the way you feel about it. Don't come to Bradford.

FRANK. Right. Now I think you ought to go to your room and look after Andrew. (*He crosses towards the door up* L.) I'm leaving.

MILLIE (*following* FRANK). What is this? Frank,

I don't understand, really I don't. What have I done?

FRANK. I think you know what you've done, Millie. Go and look after Andrew.

MILLIE (*moving to the* L. *end of the settee*). Andrew? Why this sudden concern for Andrew?

FRANK. Because I think he's just been about as badly hurt as a human being can be; and as he's a sick man and in a rather hysterical state it might be a good plan to go and see how he is.

MILLIE (*scornfully*). Hurt? Andrew hurt? You can't hurt Andrew. He's dead.

FRANK (*moving to* R. *of* MILLIE). Why do you hate him so much, Millie?

MILLIE. Because he keeps me from you.

FRANK. That isn't true.

MILLIE. Because he's not a man at all.

FRANK. He's a human being.

MILLIE. You've got a fine right to be so noble about him, after deceiving him for six months.

FRANK. Twice in six months—at your urgent invitation.

(MILLIE *slaps his face, in a violent paroxysm of rage.*)

Thank you for that. I deserved it. (*He crosses to the chair* R. *of the desk.*) I deserve a lot worse than that, too.

MILLIE (*running to him*). Frank, forgive me—I didn't mean it.

FRANK (*quietly*). You'd better have the truth, Millie, it had to come some time. (*He turns to face* MILLIE.) I've never loved you. I've never told you I loved you.

MILLIE. I know, Frank, I know. (*She backs away slightly.*) I've always accepted that.

FRANK. You asked me just now if I was running away from you. Well, I was.

MILLIE. I knew that, too.

FRANK. But I was coming to Bradford. It was going to be the very last time I was ever going to see you and at Bradford I would have told you that.

MILLIE. You wouldn't. You wouldn't. You've tried to tell me that so often before—(*she crosses to the fireplace*) and I've always stopped you somehow—somehow. I would have stopped you again.

FRANK (*quietly*). I don't think so, Millie. Not this time.

MILLIE (*crossing to* R. *of the table* C.). Frank, I don't care what humiliations you heap on me. I know you don't give two hoots for me as a person. I've always known that. I've never minded so long as you cared for me as a woman. And you do, Frank. You do. You do, don't you?

(FRANK *is silent. He crosses slowly to the fireplace.*)

It'll be all right at Bradford, you see. It'll be all right, there.

FRANK. I'm not coming to Bradford, Millie.

(*The door up* C. *opens slowly and* ANDREW *enters. He is carrying the bottle of medicine. He hands it to* MILLIE *and passes on crossing down* L. *below the desk.* MILLIE *holds the bottle up to the light.*)

ANDREW (*gently*). You should know me well enough by now, my dear, to realize how unlikely it is that I should ever take an overdose.

(MILLIE, *without a word, puts the bottle on the sideboard and goes out up* C. ANDREW *goes to the cupboard down* L. *and takes out the sherry and one glass.*)

FRANK. I'm not staying to dinner, I'm afraid.

ANDREW. Indeed? I'm sorry to hear that. You'll have a glass of sherry?

FRANK. No, thank you.

ANDREW. You will forgive me if I do.

FRANK. Of course. Perhaps I'll change my mind. (*He crosses to* C.)

(ANDREW *takes out a second glass and fills both of them.*)

About Taplow . . .

ANDREW. Oh yes?

FRANK. It *is* perfectly true that he was imitating you. I, of course, was mostly to blame in that, and I'm very sorry.

ANDREW. That is perfectly all right. Was it a good imitation?

FRANK. No.

ANDREW. I expect it was. Boys are often very clever mimics.

FRANK. We talked about you, of course, before that. (*He moves in to* R. *of the desk.*) He said—you probably won't believe this, but I thought I ought to tell you—he said he liked you very much.

(ANDREW *smiles slightly.*)

ANDREW. Indeed? (*He drinks.*)

FRANK. I can remember very clearly his exact words. He said: "He doesn't seem to like people to like him—but in spite of that, I do—very much." (*Lightly.*) So you see it looks after all as if the book might not have been a mere question of—appeasement.

ANDREW. The book? (*He picks it up.*) Dear me! What a lot of fuss about a little book—and a not very good little book at that. (*He drops it on the desk.*)

FRANK. I would like you to believe me.

ANDREW. Possibly you would, my dear Hunter; but I can assure you I am not particularly concerned about Taplow's views of my character: or about yours either, if it comes to that.

FRANK (*hopelessly*). I think you should keep that book all the same. You may find it'll mean something to you after all.

ANDREW (*turning to the cupboard and pouring himself another sherry*). Exactly. It will mean a perpetual reminder to myself of the story with which Taplow is at this very moment regaling his friends in the House. "I gave the Crock a book, to buy him off, and he blubbed. The Crock blubbed. I tell you I was there. I saw it. The Crock blubbed." My mimicry is not as good as his, I fear. Forgive me. (*He moves up* L. *of the desk.*) And now let us leave this idiotic subject and talk of more pleasant things. Do you like this sherry? I got it on my last visit to London.

FRANK. If Taplow ever breathes a word of that story to anyone at all, I'll murder him. But he won't. And if you think I will you greatly under-estimate my character as well as his. (*He drains his glass and puts it on the desk. He moves to the door up* L.)

(ANDREW *comes down* L., *puts his glass on the cupboard, and stands facing down stage.*)

Good-bye.

ANDREW. Are you leaving so soon? Good-bye, my dear fellow.

(FRANK *stops. He takes out his cigarette case and places it on the* L. *end of the table* C.)

FRANK. As this is the last time I shall probably ever see you, I'm going to offer you a word of advice.

ANDREW (*politely*). I shall be glad to listen to it.

FRANK. Leave your wife.

(*There is a pause.* ANDREW *looks out of the window.*)

ANDREW. So that you may the more easily carry on your intrigue with her?

FRANK (*moving in to the upstage end of the desk*). How long have you known that?

ANDREW. Since it first began

FRANK. How did you find out?

ANDREW. By information.

FRANK. By whose information?

ANDREW. By someone's whose word I could hardly discredit.

(*There is a pause.*)

FRANK (*slowly, with repulsion*). No! That's too horrible to think of.

ANDREW (*turning to* FRANK). Nothing is ever too horrible to think of, Hunter. It is simply a question of facing facts.

FRANK. She might have told you a lie. Have you faced that fact?

ANDREW. She never tells me a lie. In twenty years she has never told me a lie. Only the truth.

FRANK. This was a lie.

ANDREW (*moving up* L. *of* FRANK). No, my dear Hunter. Do you wish me to quote you dates?

FRANK (*still unable to believe it*). And she told you six months ago?

ANDREW (*moving down* L.). Isn't it seven?

FRANK (*savagely*). Then why have you allowed me inside your home? Why haven't you done something—reported me to the governors—anything—made a scene, knocked me down?

ANDREW. Knocked you down?

FRANK. You didn't have to invite me to dinner.

ANDREW. My dear Hunter, if, over the last twenty years, I had allowed such petty considerations to influence my choice of dinner guests I would have found it increasingly hard to remember which master to invite and which to refuse. You see, Hunter, you mustn't flatter yourself you are the first. My information is a good deal better than yours, you understand. It's authentic.

(*There is a pause.*)

FRANK. She's evil.

ANDREW. That's hardly a kindly epithet to apply to a lady whom, I gather, you have asked to marry.

FRANK. Did she tell you that?

ANDREW. She's a dutiful wife. She tells me everything.

FRANK. That, at least, was a lie.

ANDREW. She never lies.

FRANK (*leaning on the desk*). That was a lie. Do you want the truth? Can you bear the truth?

ANDREW. I can bear anything. (*He crosses to the fireplace.*)

FRANK (*turning to face* ANDREW). What I did I did cold-bloodedly out of weakness and ignorance and crass stupidity. I'm bitterly, bitterly ashamed of myself, but, in a sense, I'm glad you know (*he moves* C.) though I'd rather a thousand times that you'd heard it from me than from your wife. I won't ask you to forgive me. I can only tell you, with complete truth, that the only emotion she has ever succeeded in arousing in me she aroused in me for the first time ten minutes ago—an intense and passionate disgust.

ANDREW. What a delightfully chivalrous statement.

FRANK (*moving below the settee*). Forget chivalry, Crock, for God's sake. Forget all your fine mosaic scruples. You must leave her—it's your only chance.

ANDREW. She's my wife, Hunter. You seem to forget that. As long as she wishes to remain my wife, she may.

FRANK. She's out to kill you.

ANDREW. My dear Hunter, if that was indeed her purpose, you should know by now that she fulfilled it long ago.

FRANK. Why won't you leave her?

ANDREW. Because I wouldn't wish to add another grave wrong to one I have already done her.

FRANK. What wrong have you done her?

ANDREW. To marry her.

(*There is a pause.* FRANK *stares at him in silence.*)

You see, my dear Hunter, she is really quite as much to be pitied as I. We are both of us interesting subjects for your microscope. (*He sits on the fender.*) Both of us needing from the other something that would make life supportable for us, and neither of us able to give it. Two kinds of love. Hers and mine. Worlds apart, as I know now, though when I married her I didn't think they were incompatible. In those days I hadn't thought that her kind of love—the love she requires and which I was unable to give her—was so important that its absence would drive out the other kind of love—the kind of love that I require and which I thought, in my folly, was by far the greater part of love. (*He rises.*) I may have been, you see, Hunter, a brilliant classical scholar, but I was woefully ignorant of the facts of life. I know better now, of course. I know that in both of us, the love that we should have borne each other has turned to bitter hatred. That's all the problem is. Not a very unusual one, I venture to think—nor nearly as tragic as you seem to imagine. Merely the problem of an unsatisfied wife and a henpecked husband. You'll find it all over the world. It is usually, I believe, a subject for farce. (*He turns to the mantelpiece and adjusts the hands of the clock.*) And now, if you have to leave us, my dear fellow, please don't let me detain you any longer.

(FRANK *makes no move to go.*)

FRANK. Don't go to Bradford. Stay here, until you take up your new job.

ANDREW. I think I've already told you I'm not interested in your advice.

FRANK. Leave her. It's the only way.

ANDREW (*violently*). Will you please go !

FRANK. All right. I'd just like you to say goodbye to me, properly, though. Will you ? I shan't see you again. I know you don't want my pity, but, I would like to be of some help.

(ANDREW *turns and faces* FRANK.)

ANDREW. If you think, by this expression of kindness, Hunter, that you can get me to repeat the shameful exhibition of emotion I made to Taplow a moment ago, I must tell you that you have no chance. My hysteria over that book just now was no more than a sort of reflex action of the spirit. The muscular twitchings of a corpse. It can never happen again.

FRANK. A corpse can be revived.

ANDREW. I don't believe in miracles.

FRANK. Don't you? Funnily enough, as a scientist, I do.

ANDREW (*turning to the fireplace*). Your faith would be touching, if I were capable of being touched by it.

FRANK. You are, I think. (*He moves behind* ANDREW. *After a pause.*) I'd like to come and visit you at this crammer's.

ANDREW. That is an absurd suggestion.

FRANK. I suppose it is rather, but all the same I'd like to do it. May I?

ANDREW. Of course not.

FRANK (*sitting on the settee*). Your term begins on the first of September, doesn't it? (*He takes out a pocket diary.*)

ANDREW. I tell you the idea is quite childish.

FRANK. I could come about the second week.

ANDREW. You would be bored to death. So, probably, would I.

FRANK (*glancing at his diary*). Let's say Monday the twelfth, then.

ANDREW (*turning to face* FRANK, *his hands beginning to tremble*). Say anything you like, only please go. Please go, Hunter.

FRANK (*writing in his book and not looking at* ANDREW). That's fixed, then. Monday, September the twelfth. Will you remember that?

ANDREW (*after a pause; with difficulty*). I suppose I'm at least as likely to remember it as you are.

FRANK. That's fixed, then. (*He rises, slips the book into his pocket and puts out his hand.*) Good-bye, until then. (*He moves in to* ANDREW.)

(ANDREW *hesitates, then shakes his hand.*)

ANDREW. Good-bye.

FRANK. May I go out through your garden? (*He crosses to* C.)

ANDREW (*nodding*). Of course.

FRANK. I'm off to have a quick word with Taplow. By the way, may I take him a message from you?

ANDREW. What message?

FRANK. Has he or has he not got his remove?

ANDREW. He has.

FRANK. May I tell him?

ANDREW. It is highly irregular. Yes, you may.

FRANK. Good. (*He turns to go, then turns back.*) Oh, by the way, I'd better have the address of that crammer's. (*He moves below the settee, takes out his diary, and points his pencil, ready to write.*)

(MILLIE *enters up* C. *She carries a casserole on three plates.*)

MILLIE (*coming above the table* C.). Dinner's ready. You're staying, Frank, aren't you? (*She puts the casserole and plates on the table.*)

FRANK (*politely*). No. I'm afraid not. (*To* ANDREW.) What's that address?

ANDREW (*after great hesitation*). The Old Deanery, Malcombe, Dorset.

FRANK. I'll write to you and you can let me know about trains. Good-bye. (*To* MILLIE.) Good-bye.

(*He crosses to the door up* L. *and goes out.* MILLIE *is silent for a moment. Then she laughs.*)

MILLIE. That's a laugh, I must say.

ANDREW. What's a laugh, my dear?

MILLIE. You inviting him to stay with you.

ANDREW. I didn't. He suggested it.

MILLIE (*moving to the* L. *end of the settee*). He's coming to Bradford.

ANDREW. Yes. I remember your telling me so.

MILLIE. He's coming to Bradford. He's not going to you.

ANDREW. The likeliest contingency is, that he's not going to either of us.

MILLIE. He's coming to Bradford.

ANDREW. I expect so. Oh, by the way, I'm not. I shall be staying here until I go to Dorset.

MILLIE (*indifferently*). Suit yourself. What makes you think I'll join you there?

ANDREW. I don't.

MILLIE. You needn't expect me.

ANDREW. I don't think either of us has the right to expect anything further from the other.

(*The telephone rings.*)

Excuse me. (*He moves to the table down* R. *and lifts the receiver.*) Hullo . . .

(*While he is speaking* MILLIE *crosses to* L. *of the table* C. *About to sit, she sees the cigarette case. She picks it up, fingers it for a moment, and finally drops it into her pocket.*)

Yes, Headmaster . . . The time-table? . . . It's perfectly simple. The middle fourth B division will take a ten-minute break on Tuesdays and a fifteen-minute break on alternate Wednesdays; while exactly the reverse procedure will apply to the lower Shell, C division. I thought I had sufficiently explained that on my chart . . . Oh, I see . . . Thank you, that is very good of you . . . Yes. I think you will find it will work out quite satisfactorily . . . Oh by the way, Headmaster. I have changed my mind about the prize-giving ceremony. I intend to speak after, instead of before, Fletcher, as is my privilege . . . Yes, I quite understand, but I am now seeing the matter in a different light . . . I know, but I am of opinion that occasionally an anti-climax can be surprisingly effective. Good-bye. (*He replaces the receiver, crosses to* R. *of the table* C., *and sits.*) Come along, my dear. We mustn't let our dinner get cold. (*He unrolls his table napkin.*)

MILLIE *sits* L. *of the table and unrolls her table napkin.* ANDREW *offers her the bread. She ignores it. He takes a piece. She removes the lid of the casserole as—*

the CURTAIN *falls.*

FURNITURE AND PROPERTY PLOT

FURNITURE AND PROPERTY PLOT

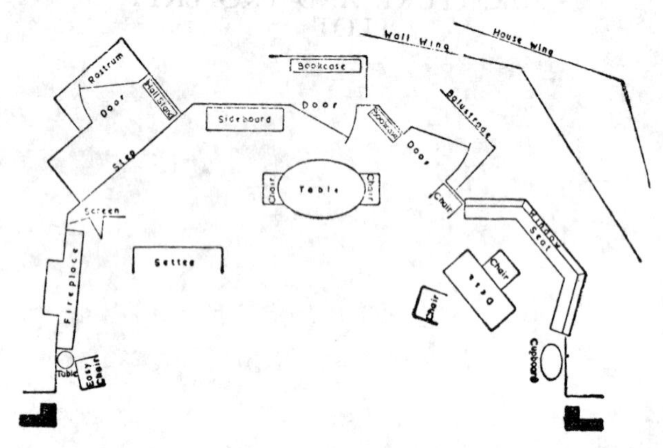

On Stage.

Desk. *On it:* blotter, inkstand, pens, pencils, envelopes, notepaper, spectacles (spare), exercise books, copy of *The Agamemnon*, ashtray, cigarette box, notes on speech, books for dressing. *In drawer:* scissors.

Swivel chair.

Cupboard, down L. *In it:* bottle of sherry, 4 glasses.
On it: ornament.

Oval table, C. *On it:* bowl of flowers, ashtray, box of chocolates.

Bookcase.

Sideboard. *On it:* cigarette box.

Hall-stand. *In it:* 2 walking-sticks.

Settee. *On it:* copy of *The Times*, copy of the *Tatler*.

Screen.

Fender.

Occasional table, down R. *On it:* telephone, ashtray.

Easy chair.

On mantelpiece: clock, 4 ornaments, ashtray, snuffbox.

Off Stage R.

Exercise-book, school book, copy of *The Agamemnon*, pen (TAPLOW).

Shopping basket containing copy of the *Tatler*, prescription, luggage labels, purse with shilling, various pieces of shopping (MILLIE).

Cape (MILLIE).
Mackintosh, time-table (ANDREW).
Medicine bottle (TAPLOW).

Off Stage C.
Apron (MILLIE).
Tray with 3 glasses, cruet, 3 knives, 3 forks, tablespoon, glass, bread basket, 3 table napkins (2 with rings), 3 table mats, 1 large table mat (MILLIE).
Casserole on 3 dinner-plates (MILLIE).

Personal.
FRANK: cigarette case, lighter, diary.
ANDREW: spectacles, pocket watch.
FROBISHER: pocket watch.

MADE AND PRINTED IN GREAT BRITAIN BY
LATIMER TREND & COMPANY LTD PLYMOUTH